easy cookies

easy cookies

Linda Collister

photography by Diana Miller

RYLAND
PETERS
& SMALL

LONDON NEW YORK

First published in USA in 2005
by Ryland Peters & Small, Inc.
519 Broadway, 5th Floor
New York, NY 10012
www.rylandpeters.com

10 9 8 7 6 5 4 3 2 1

Library of Congress Cataloging-in-
Publication Data

Collister, Linda.
  Easy cookies / Linda Collister ;
photography by Diana Miller.
     p. cm.
  Includes index.
  ISBN 1-84172-952-3
  1. Cookies. I. Title.

TX772.C385 2005
641.8'654--dc22
                              2005000775

Dedication
To Emily, Daniel, and Stevie.

Acknowledgments
I would to thank the many people who
helped with this book; Elsa Petersen-
Schepelern, Steve Painter, Diana Miller,
Róisín Nield, Barbara Levy, Simon
Silverwood, and Alan Hertz.

Senior Designer Steve Painter
Commissioning Editor
   Elsa Petersen-Schepelern
Editor Susan Stuck
Production Patricia Harrington
Art Director Gabriella Le Grazie
Publishing Director Alison Starling

Food Stylist Linda Collister
Prop Stylist Róisín Nield

contents

introduction

Few of us can resist a cookie warm from the oven; add a glass of milk or a cup of coffee or tea and you have pure, simple pleasure.

Since you can't make just one, and you really shouldn't eat the whole batch yourself, home-baked cookies are ideal for sharing. They are adaptable, too: luckily there is no "proper" time of day to eat a cookie, no rules that say you can't eat cheese crackers with soup or chocolate cookies with ice cream.

The other delight of cookies is their simplicity: a few ingredients, easy assembly, and rapid baking. The key to success is good materials like unsalted butter, free-range eggs, sugar, fresh flour. Buy organic if you can. For some recipes the eggs and butter should be used at room temperature rather than straight from the refrigerator.

Nuts and chocolate are key ingredients for many recipes; the flavor of the final result will depend on their quality. Nuts turn rancid very quickly, so buy in small quantities and use a fresh package (after opening, wrap the rest of the package tightly and store in the freezer). Buy the best chocolate you can afford—these days there is a good range at most supermarkets (even excellent Fairtrade chocolate). It's worth trying out a few small bars to find the one you really enjoy.

These cookies are easy to prepare, but for some recipes an electric mixer or food processor will speed up the beating, mixing, or chopping.

Other equipment is quite basic, but a good, heavy-duty baking sheet is invaluable. I've been using mine on an almost daily basis for 20 years, so it has repaid the initial investment. My son now wants one of his own.

It is very convenient to have a large wire cooling rack, though you can also use the rack from the broiler pan or an oven shelf. An airtight container for storing your cookies will be useful too, while many of the cookies can be frozen.

You need a good, reliable oven. It is worth getting an inexpensive oven thermometer to double-check the temperature, plus a kitchen timer: thermostats and clocks, even on the best of ovens, can be unreliable. The cooking times are guidelines; your oven handbook and your own oven knowledge will teach you which shelf works best, and baking times should be reduced for convection ovens.

In this book, you'll find all sorts of cookies and crackers—the chunky All-American; the thin and crispy Continental; the rich, buttery Scottish shortbread. I can't ever decide on a favorite; it all depends on the weather.

classics

These cookies are always popular, whether plain or flavored with dried fruit or spices. Use old-fashioned oatmeal or rolled oats rather than "instant."

classic oat cookies

1 stick unsalted butter, very soft

¾ cup firmly packed light brown sugar

1 extra-large egg, beaten

1 tablespoon milk

½ teaspoon pure vanilla extract

¾ cup plus 1 tablespoon self-rising flour

1½ cups coarse oatmeal or rolled oats

2 baking sheets, very lightly greased

Makes 24

Put the butter, sugar, egg, milk, and vanilla in a bowl and beat well using an electric mixer or a wooden spoon. Add the flour and oats and mix well with the wooden spoon.

Put heaping teaspoons of dough onto the prepared pans, spacing them well apart.

Bake in a preheated oven at 350°F for 12–15 minutes until lightly browned around the edges.

Let cool in the pan for 2 minutes, then transfer to a wire rack to cool completely.

Store in an airtight container and eat within 5 days or freeze for up to a month.

Variations At the same time as the flour, add either:
- ½ cup dried fruit (raisins, cherries, cranberries, or blueberries)
- 1 teaspoon ground cinnamon, 1 teaspoon apple pie spice, and 2 pinches of ground black pepper
- ⅓ cup chocolate chips and ¼ cup chopped almonds.

For the best flavor, use an all-natural peanut butter with no added sugar or fat. The crunchy coating is made by rolling the cookie mixture in roasted (but unsalted) peanuts before baking.

extra-crunchy peanut butter cookies

1 stick unsalted butter, softened

½ cup crunchy peanut butter

¾ cup firmly packed light brown sugar

1 extra-large egg, lightly beaten

½ teaspoon pure vanilla extract

1½ cups self-rising flour

1⅓ cups roasted unsalted peanut halves

2 baking sheets, greased

Makes 20

Put the soft butter, peanut butter, sugar, beaten egg, vanilla, and flour in a large bowl. Mix well with a wooden spoon. When thoroughly combined, take walnut-size portions of the dough (about a tablespoon) and roll into balls with your hands. Put the peanut halves in a shallow dish, then roll the dough in the nuts. Arrange the balls well apart on the prepared pans, then gently flatten slightly with your fingers.

Bake in a preheated oven at 350°F for 12–15 minutes until light golden brown.

Let cool in the pan for a couple of minutes to firm up, then transfer to a wire rack to cool completely.

Store in an airtight container and eat within 5 days or freeze for up to a month.

The classic recipe is three parts flour, two parts butter, and one part sugar, with some of the flour replaced with rice flour, ground rice, or cornstarch to give the traditional light, short, and sandy texture. The better the butter you use, the finer the flavor and texture—a well-salted, cheap, blended butter will make the shortbread heavier. Shortbread can be thinly rolled and cut into disks, or pressed into a shallow cake pan to make the usual thicker "petticoat tails."

scottish shortbread

2 cups all-purpose flour

⅓ cup rice flour, ground rice, or cornstarch

½ cup sugar, plus a little extra for sprinkling

1¾ sticks unsalted butter, chilled and cut into small pieces

a shallow round cake pan, about 9 inches in diameter, lightly greased

or a 3-inch fluted round cookie cutter and 2 baking sheets, greased

Makes about 20 rounds or 12 petticoat tails

Put the all-purpose flour, rice flour (or ground rice, or cornstarch), and sugar in a food processor. Process until thoroughly mixed. Add the pieces of butter and process until the ingredients come together to make a ball of dough. Carefully remove the dough from the machine.

If making petticoat tails, lightly flour your fingers, then gently press the dough into the cake pan to make an even layer. Prick all over with a fork, then gently score the mixture into 12 wedges using a sharp, pointed knife.

If making thin rounds, roll out the dough on a lightly floured work surface with a floured rolling pin to about ¼ inch thick and cut out rounds with the cookie cutter. Gently knead the trimmings, then re-roll and cut out more rounds. Set the rounds slightly apart on the prepared pans. Prick with a fork.

Chill the shortbread for 15 minutes, then bake in a preheated oven at 350°F for 15–20 minutes for the petticoat tails, and 10–12 minutes for the rounds, until just firm and barely colored. Sprinkle the shortbread with a little sugar, then let cool for 2 minutes.

For petticoat tails, cut the segments along the marked lines, then leave until cold before removing from the pan. For the rounds, transfer to a wire rack to cool completely.

Store in an airtight container and eat within a week or freeze for up to a month.

I've been eating and making these cookies since I could walk. The recipe comes from my grandmother, and is now a favorite with a fourth generation.

gingerbread cookies

⅓ cup self-rising flour

a pinch of salt

1 cup sugar,
plus extra for sprinkling

2 teaspoons ground ginger

2 teaspoons ground cinnamon

1 teaspoon baking soda

1 stick unsalted butter

¼ cup molasses

1 extra-large egg, beaten

2–3 baking sheets, greased

Makes 30

Sift the flour, salt, sugar, ginger, cinnamon, and baking soda into a large bowl. Heat the butter and molasses very gently in a small saucepan until melted.

Pour onto the dry ingredients, add the beaten egg, and mix thoroughly with a wooden spoon. Using your hands, roll the dough into 30 walnut-size balls. Arrange well apart on the prepared pans, then flatten slightly with your fingers. Sprinkle with a little sugar, then bake in a preheated oven at 325°F for 12–15 minutes or until firm and lightly browned. Remove from the oven and let cool in the pan for 2 minutes. Transfer to a wire rack to cool completely.

Store in an airtight container and eat within 5 days or freeze for up to a month.

Variation To make Candied Ginger Cookies, replace the molasses with light corn syrup. Finely chop 2 pieces of candied ginger and add with the egg.

Parkin is a kind of sticky gingerbread from Yorkshire, England, made with oatmeal, molasses, and spice. These cookies are made from the same ingredients and have the same flavor and a crunchy texture.

parkin cookies

¾ cup plus 2 tablespoons self-rising flour

¾ cup fine oatmeal

1 teaspoon ground ginger

½ teaspoon ground allspice

3 tablespoons dark brown sugar

6 tablespoons unsalted butter

2 tablespoons light corn syrup

1 tablespoon molasses

confectioners' sugar, for dusting (optional)

2 baking sheets, greased

Makes 20

Put the flour, oatmeal, ginger, allspice, and sugar in a large bowl and mix well. Make a hollow in the center.

Put the butter, light corn syrup, and molasses in a small saucepan and heat gently until melted.

Pour the mixture into the hollow in the dry ingredients and mix well with a wooden spoon. Using floured hands, take walnut-size portions of the dough (about a tablespoon) and roll into balls. Set well apart on the prepared pans. Bake in a preheated oven at 350°F for 15 minutes until firm.

Let cool on the trays for 2 minutes to firm up, then transfer to a wire rack to cool completely. Serve dusted with confectioners' sugar, if using.

Store in an airtight container and eat within 5 days or freeze for up to a month.

Note Fine oatmeal can be found in the organic and natural food section of many supermarkets (next to coarse oatmeal, used to make hot oatmeal). If you can't find it, put regular coarse oatmeal in a food processor and grind until fine. You can also use oatbran, available in supermarkets.

The rich, soft dough should be thoroughly chilled before being sliced and baked. The dough can be stored in the refrigerator for up to a week, or frozen for up to a month before finishing the recipe. The result is a melt-in-the-mouth cookie.

icebox cookies

1½ sticks unsalted butter, at room temperature

¾ cup confectioners' sugar, sifted

1 teaspoon pure vanilla extract

1 cup old-fashioned oatmeal or rolled oats

½ teaspoon baking powder

1⅔ cups all-purpose flour

sugar, for sprinkling

2 baking sheets, greased

Makes about 18

Put the soft butter and confectioners' sugar in a large bowl and beat with a wooden spoon or electric mixer on low speed, until light and fluffy. Beat in the vanilla, then stir in the oats.

Sift the baking powder and flour into the bowl, then mix with your hands or a wooden spoon to make a slightly soft but not sticky dough.

Shape the dough into a log about 3 inches in diameter, then wrap thoroughly in plastic wrap or wax paper. Chill until firm—at least 30 minutes or up to a week. The dough can be frozen for up to a month, then defrosted in the refrigerator for 12 hours.

Slice the log into rounds about ¼ inch thick, then arrange slightly apart on the prepared pans. Sprinkle lightly with the sugar.

Bake in a preheated oven at 325°F for 15–20 minutes until lightly golden around the edges.

Let cool on the tray for 2 minutes, then transfer to a wire rack to cool completely.

Store in an airtight container and eat within 5 days or freeze for up to a month.

Variation Before baking the cookies, sprinkle the top of each one with about ⅓ cup chocolate chips or about 1½ oz. grated semisweet chocolate.

For a real taste of Normandy, use their delicious unsalted butter. The dough is made in a processor, rolled out, then cut into pretty fluted discs or shaped into a log and sliced into rounds. The tops of the cookies are brushed with egg to give a rich, glossy finish, then patterned with a fork.

french sablés

1½ cups all-purpose flour

a pinch of salt

⅔ cup confectioners' sugar

10 tablespoons unsalted butter, chilled and cut into small pieces

3 extra-large egg yolks

½ teaspoon pure vanilla extract

1 egg, beaten, to glaze

a fluted cookie cutter, 3½ inches in diameter

2–3 baking sheets, greased

Makes about 10

Put the flour, salt, sugar, and pieces of butter in a food processor. Process until the mixture looks like fine crumbs. Add the egg yolks and vanilla and process again until the mixture comes together to make a firm dough. Remove from the processor.

To make the rolled out cookies, wrap the dough well in plastic wrap, then chill for 30 minutes or until firm. Roll out the chilled dough on a lightly floured work surface to about ¼ inch thick. Cut out rounds with the fluted cutter and arrange them slightly apart on the prepared pans. Knead the trimmings together, roll again, and cut out more rounds.

To make sliced cookies, shape the dough into a log about 6 x 8 cm. Wrap and chill for 1 hour or until very firm. The dough can be kept in the refrigerator for up to 2 days. Using a large, sharp knife, slice the dough into rounds about ¼ inch thick and arrange them slightly apart on the prepared pans, 4–5 on each pan.

Brush the rounds very lightly with beaten egg, then chill for 15 minutes.

Brush again with beaten egg, prick all over with a fork, then mark with the prongs to make a neat pattern.

Bake in a preheated oven at 350°F for 12–15 minutes or until golden brown.

Let cool on the trays for 2 minutes, then transfer to a wire rack to cool completely. Store in an airtight container and eat within a week or freeze for up to a month.

chocolate

Always popular and hard to beat! I've adapted the classic recipe so that it uses less sugar and more nuts. Use semisweet chocolate broken up into chunks or a bag of chocolate chips.

classic chocolate chip cookies

1⅓ cups self-rising flour

a pinch of salt

a good pinch of baking soda

1 stick unsalted butter, very soft

⅓ cup minus 1 tablespoon sugar

⅓ cup lightly packed light brown sugar

½ teaspoon real vanilla extract

1 extra-large egg, lightly beaten

1 cup semi-sweet chocolate chips

¾ cup walnut or pecan pieces

2 baking sheets, greased

Makes 24

Put all the ingredients in a large bowl and mix thoroughly with a wooden spoon.

Drop heaping teaspoons of the mixture onto the prepared pans, spacing them well apart.

Bake in a preheated oven at 375°F for 8–10 minutes until lightly colored and just firm.

Let cool on the pans for a minute, then transfer to a wire rack to cool completely.

Store in an airtight container and eat within 5 days or freeze for up to a month.

The original mocha was a fine Arabian coffee shipped from a port in Yemen called Mocha. Now the word means either a hot drink made of coffee and chocolate together, or other sweet mixtures using these two flavors. These little cookies are perfect with a cup of coffee after dinner.

mocha kisses

1⅓ cups self-rising flour

½ cup sugar

6 tablespoons unsalted butter, chilled and cut into small pieces

1 extra-large egg

2 teaspoons instant coffee granules or powder

Filling

5 tablespoons unsalted butter, very soft

1¼ cups confectioners' sugar

2 teaspoons instant coffee granules or powder

2 teaspoons unsweetened cocoa

2 baking sheets, greased

Makes 9

If making the dough by hand, mix the flour and sugar in a bowl. Add the pieces of butter and, using the tips of your fingers, rub in until the mixture looks like breadcrumbs. Put the coffee in a bowl and dissolve in 1 teaspoon of warm water. Add the egg and beat lightly. Stir the egg and coffee mixture into the flour mixture with a wooden spoon. Mix well so that the ingredients come together to make a firm dough.

If making the dough in a food processor, put the flour, sugar, and pieces of butter in the bowl of the machine. Process until the mixture looks like breadcrumbs. Add the egg, then the coffee dissolved in 1 teaspoon of warm water. Process until the dough comes together.

Flour your hands and roll the dough into 18 walnut-size balls. Arrange them slightly apart on the prepared pans and bake in a preheated oven at 325°F for 10–15 minutes until a light golden color.

Remove from the oven, let cool on the tray for 2 minutes, then transfer them to a wire rack to cool completely.

Meanwhile, to make the filling, put the soft butter, sugar, coffee, and cocoa in a bowl and beat well with a wooden spoon or electric mixer or whisk—there will be flecks of coffee in the smooth frosting. Use the mixture to sandwich the cookies in pairs.

Store in an airtight container and eat within 24 hours. Not suitable for freezing.

Variation To make Coffee Walnut Kisses, make the filling without the cocoa. Stir in 3 tablespoons chopped walnuts and use the crunchy coffee walnut frosting to sandwich the cookies.

Good-quality semisweet chocolate is used in these cookies both as chunks and as a powder (by simply processing with the flour).

double chocolate pecans

1 cup old-fashioned oatmeal or rolled oats (not instant)

1¼ cups all-purpose flour

½ teaspoon baking powder

½ teaspoon baking soda

½ cup firmly packed light brown sugar

7 oz. semisweet chocolate, broken up

1 stick unsalted butter, very soft

1 extra-large egg, beaten

1 cup pecan pieces

2 baking sheets, greased

Makes 24

Put the oats in a food processor. Add the flour, baking powder, baking soda, the sugar, and half of the chocolate pieces. Process until the mixture has a sandy texture.

Put the soft butter, beaten egg, pecan pieces, and the remaining pieces of chocolate in a large bowl. Add the mixture from the processor and mix well with a wooden spoon or your hands to make a firm dough.

Roll walnut-size pieces of dough into balls using your hands. Arrange well apart on the prepared pans and flatten slightly with the back of a fork. Bake in a preheated oven at 375°F for 12–15 minutes until almost firm.

Let cool on the trays for 2 minutes, then transfer to a wire rack to cool completely.

Store in an airtight container and eat within 5 days or freeze for up to a month.

A simple melt-and-mix recipe, best made with very good semisweet chocolate—no baking needed. The result is a really rich chocolate cookie, ideal with coffee after a meal.

chilled chocolate squares

9 tablespoons unsalted butter

3 tablespoons light corn syrup

7 oz. good quality semisweet chocolate, broken up

½ cup nuts (whole almonds, hazelnuts, walnuts, or a mixture)

3 tablespoons dried cherries or cranberries

⅓ cup raisins

15–16 plain crisp cookies, such as Petit Beurre

a jelly roll pan or shallow baking pan about 12 x 8 inches, lined with nonstick parchment paper

Makes 24

Put the butter, syrup, and chocolate in a heatproof bowl. Set the bowl over a saucepan of gently simmering water and melt gently, stirring frequently.

Remove the bowl from the pan and add the whole nuts, cherries, and raisins.

Break up the cookies into pieces the size of your thumbnail and add to the bowl. Mix gently with a wooden spoon.

When thoroughly mixed, transfer to the prepared pan and spread evenly. Chill until firm, about 2 hours.

Cut into 24 squares and remove from the pan. Serve chilled. Store in the refrigerator in an airtight container for up to a week.

Variations
- For the holidays, soak the raisins in 2 tablespoons brandy for 1–2 hours before using.
- For children, replace the dried cherries with mini marshmallows.

A very quick, rich recipe using chocolate and a food processor. Good served with ice cream.

chocolate fudge cookies

⅓ cup sugar

½ cup firmly packed light brown sugar

5 oz. good semisweet chocolate, broken up

1 stick unsalted butter, chilled and cut into small pieces

1¼ cups all-purpose flour

½ teaspoon baking powder

1 extra-large egg, lightly beaten

2 baking sheets, greased

Makes about 20

Put both the sugars in a food processor. Add the pieces of chocolate, then process until the mixture has a sandy texture.

Add the pieces of butter, flour, baking powder, and egg and process until the mixture comes together to make a firm dough. Carefully remove from the machine.

Using lightly floured hands, roll the dough into about 20 walnut-size balls. Arrange the balls, spaced well apart, on the prepared pans.

Bake in a preheated oven at 350°F for 12–15 minutes until firm.

Let cool on the trays for 2 minutes, then transfer to wire racks to cool completely.

Store in an airtight container and eat within 5 days or freeze for up to a month.

Variation Remove the dough from the processor and work in ½ cup pecan pieces, then shape and bake the cookies as above.

Just a few drops of Tabasco gives these moist and rich cookies a fascinating, subtle flavor. Ask your friends if they can guess the mystery ingredient.

macadamia and white chocolate chile cookies

1¼ cups macadamia nuts

1⅔ cups all-purpose flour

½ teaspoon baking powder

⅔ cup firmly packed light brown sugar

1 stick unsalted butter, very soft

1 extra-large egg, lightly beaten

5 drops Tabasco

3½ oz. white chocolate, broken into chunks, or chips

2 baking sheets, greased

Makes 20

Put the nuts in an ovenproof dish and toast in a preheated oven at 350°F for 5–7 minutes until light golden brown. Let cool, then chop coarsely by hand or in a food processor. Leave the oven on.

Put the chopped nuts, flour, baking powder, sugar, butter, egg, Tabasco, and chocolate pieces in a large bowl and mix thoroughly with a wooden spoon.

Using about a tablespoon of the mixture for each cookie, drop each spoonful onto the prepared pans, spacing well apart.

Bake in the heated oven for 12–15 minutes until light golden brown.

Let cool on the trays for 2 minutes, then transfer to a wire rack to cool completely.

Store in an airtight container and eat within 4 days or freeze for up to a month.

These dark, dark chocolate cookies have a white "crazy-paving" top. The effect is created by rolling the cookies in confectioners' sugar just before baking. The surface then cracks to form the "paving."

chocolate crackle cookies

3 ½ oz. semisweet chocolate, broken up

1 stick unsalted butter, cut into small pieces

1 cup firmly packed light brown sugar

1 extra-large egg, beaten

2–3 drops pure vanilla extract

1 ⅓ cups self-rising flour

½ teaspoon baking soda

2 tablespoons confectioners' sugar

2 baking sheets, greased

Makes 24

Put the chocolate, butter, and sugar in a heatproof bowl and set over a saucepan of gently steaming water. Melt gently, stirring occasionally until smooth.

Remove the bowl from the pan and let cool for a minute. Stir in the egg, vanilla, flour, and baking soda and mix well.

Cover the bowl and chill until firm, about 20 minutes.

Put the confectioners' sugar in a shallow dish. Using your hands, roll the dough into walnut-size balls, then roll in the confectioners' sugar to coat thoroughly. Set the balls on the prepared pans, spacing them well apart. Bake in a preheated oven at 400°F for 10–12 minutes until just set.

Let cool on the tray for 2 minutes, then transfer to a wire rack to cool completely.

Store in an airtight container and eat within 5 days or freeze for up to a month.

celebration

These unusual cookies, made with the same rich ingredients used for a traditional British Christmas cake, come from Williamsburg. For speed, use a bag of mixed dried fruit (raisins, golden raisins, and currants) or the "luxury" type, which includes cherries, and a ready-chopped mix of nuts like Brazils, walnuts, almonds, and hazelnuts.

christmas cake cookies

1⅔ cups self-rising flour

⅛ teaspoon grated nutmeg

½ teaspoon apple pie spice

⅔ cup firmly packed dark brown sugar

1 stick unsalted butter, chilled and cut into small pieces

2 large eggs, beaten

2 tablespoons sweet sherry, brandy, or milk

1 cup chopped mixed nuts

1 cup mixed dried fruit (raisins, golden raisins, and currants)

soft brown sugar, for sprinkling

2 baking sheets, greased

Makes 20

Sift the flour, nutmeg, and apple pie spice into a large bowl. Stir in the sugar. Add the pieces of butter and rub into the flour using the tips of your fingers until the mixture looks like coarse crumbs. You can also cut the butter into the flour using a knife or special pastry cutter. Add the eggs, sherry, nuts, and dried fruit to the bowl and mix thoroughly with a wooden spoon.

Drop tablespoons of the mixture onto the prepared pans, spacing them well apart. Flatten them slightly with the back of a fork and sprinkle lightly with soft brown sugar.

Bake in a preheated oven at 350°F for 12–15 minutes, until golden.

Let cool for 2 minutes to firm up, then transfer to a cooling rack to cool completely.

Store in an airtight container and eat within 5 days, or freeze for up to a month.

Pecans, grown in a belt that runs across the South, are by far the most important and most popular nuts in North America, and were particularly prized by Algonquin Indians, who gave them their name *paccan*. In the South, pecans are used to enrich stuffings, breads, cakes, salads, and cookies as well as baked in pies—I found these rich and crumbly cookies on a visit to New Mexico.

santa fe wedding cookies

1 cup all-purpose flour

¼ cup light brown sugar

7 tablespoons unsalted butter, very soft

½ teaspoon pure vanilla extract

½ cup pecan pieces, coarsely chopped

20 pecan halves, to decorate

confectioners' sugar, to dust

2 baking sheets, greased

Makes 20

Put the flour, sugar, soft butter, vanilla, and pecans in a bowl. Using a wooden spoon, work the ingredients until they come together to form a soft dough.

Using your hands, lightly floured, roll the mixture into 20 walnut-size balls. Arrange them slightly apart on the prepared pans, then gently press a pecan half on top of each cookie. Bake in a preheated oven at 350°F for 10–12 minutes until a light golden color with slightly brown edges.

Remove from the oven and let cool in the pan for 2 minutes, then transfer to a wire rack and let cool completely. Dust with plenty of confectioners' sugar before serving. Handle carefully—these cookies are fragile.

Store in an airtight container and eat within 5 days, or freeze for up to a month.

I've adapted a very old recipe that became famous because it was written by Sinclair Lewis, the Nobel and Pulitzer prize-winning author of *Elmer Gantry*. The bourbon adds an exotic and festive tang.

sinclair lewis's christmas cookies

1 stick unsalted butter, very soft

½ cup sugar

1 extra-large egg, lightly beaten

¾ cup all-purpose flour

a pinch of salt

3 tablespoons unsweetened cocoa powder

1 tablespoon bourbon or milk

⅓ cup almonds, sliced, slivered, shredded, chopped, or flaked

2 baking sheets, greased

Makes about 24

Put the soft butter and sugar in a bowl and beat with an electric whisk or mixer, or a wooden spoon, until creamy. Gradually beat in the egg.

Sift the flour, salt, and cocoa into the bowl. Add the bourbon and almonds and mix well with a wooden spoon.

Using a heaping teaspoon of mixture for each cookie, spoon the mixture in mounds onto the prepared pans, spacing well apart.

Bake in a preheated oven at 325°F for 10–12 minutes, until firm but not colored.

Let cool on the trays for 2 minutes, then transfer to a wire rack to cool completely.

Store in an airtight container and eat within 4 days or freeze for up to a month.

Make edible Christmas decorations by cutting the spicy shortbread-like dough into tree, star, or bell shapes. After baking, decorate with ready-made frosting pens and silver balls and thread with ribbons for hanging.

german honey spice cookies

1¼ cups all-purpose flour

1 teaspoon ground cinnamon

¼ teaspoon ground ginger

¼ teaspoon apple pie spice

6 tablespoons unsalted butter, chilled and cut into small pieces

3 tablespoons honey

To finish (optional)

thin ribbon, for hanging

edible frosting writing pens

silver balls

shaped cookie cutters

2 baking sheets, greased

Makes about 12

Put the flour, cinnamon, ginger, and apple pie spice in a food processor. Add the pieces of butter and blend until the mixture looks like crumbs. Add the honey and blend again until it comes together to make a soft dough.

Remove the dough from the processor, wrap in plastic wrap or wax paper, and chill for 30 minutes or until firm.

Lightly flour the work surface and a rolling pin, then roll out the dough to about ¼ inch thick. Cut out shapes with the cookie cutters. If making as Christmas decorations, use a toothpick to pierce a hole at the top of each shape large enough to thread a thin ribbon through it.

Arrange the shapes slightly apart on the prepared pans and chill for 10 minutes. Bake in a preheated oven at 350°F for about 10 minutes until golden. Let cool for 5 minutes, then transfer to a wire rack to cool completely.

When cold, leave plain or thread with ribbon, decorate with ready-made frosting (in writing pens) and silver balls, leave until set, then hang them on the Christmas tree.

Best eaten within 24 hours if used as decorations, or store in an airtight container and eat within 4 days. Undecorated cookies can be frozen for up to a month.

Brigitte, a friend from Berlin, always makes these attractive sticky squares to celebrate the first Sunday in Advent (to mark the four weeks before Christmas).

honey and almond squares

1⅓ cups all-purpose flour

1 stick unsalted butter, chilled and cut into small pieces

2 tablespoons sugar

1 egg yolk

½ teaspoon pure vanilla extract

Topping

1½ cups slivered almonds

6 tablespoons unsalted butter

3 tablespoons sugar

2 tablespoons spreadable honey

2 tablespoons cream (light or heavy)

a jelly roll pan or shallow baking pan about 12 x 8 inches, greased

Makes 32

To make the base, put the flour, pieces of butter, sugar, egg yolk, and vanilla extract in a food processor. Blend until the mixture just comes together to make a smooth, firm dough. The ingredients can also be put in a large bowl and worked together by hand.

Transfer the dough to the prepared pan and press over the base of the pan with floured fingers to make an even layer. Prick the dough base all over with a fork, then chill for 10 minutes. Meanwhile, preheat the oven to 375°F.

Bake the dough base in the heated oven for 10–12 minutes until firm and golden. Remove from the oven (don't turn the oven off) and let cool while making the topping.

To make the topping, put the almonds, butter, sugar, and honey in a nonstick frying pan, or wide, heavy saucepan. Cook over low heat, stirring constantly with a wooden spoon, until a pale straw color. Stir in the cream and cook for 10 seconds. Remove the pan from the heat and pour the mixture over the cooked base. Spread evenly, then bake for 10 minutes until a good golden color.

Let cool in the pan, then cut into small squares. Store in an airtight container and eat within 5 days. Not suitable for freezing.

This recipe for snowy-white, rich almond cookies comes from a Czech friend, but I've eaten Polish, German, and Dutch versions, and my mother-in-law makes something similar during Hannukah.

czech almond crescents

1 cup whole blanched almonds

½ cup confectioners' sugar, plus extra for dusting

1 stick unsalted butter, chilled and cut into small pieces

2–3 drops pure almond extract

¾ cup all-purpose flour

2 baking sheets, well-greased

Makes 24

Put the almonds and sugar in a food processor and blend until the mixture becomes a fine, sandy powder.

Add the butter, almond extract, and flour and process until the mixture forms a ball of smooth dough.

Carefully remove the dough from the machine, wrap in plastic wrap, and chill for about 20 minutes or until firm. The dough can be stored in the refrigerator for 24 hours.

When ready to finish, preheat the oven to 325°F. Take a heaping teaspoon of dough and roll it with your hands to make a sausage shape about 3 inches long. Curve the dough into a crescent and set on a prepared pan. Repeat with the rest of the dough, arranging the crescents well apart on the pans.

Bake in the heated oven for 15–18 minutes until the edges are barely colored. Let cool on the trays for 2 minutes, then carefully transfer to a wire rack to cool completely. Just before serving, dust with plenty of confectioners' sugar.

Store in an airtight container and eat within a week. These cookies are fragile and, while they can be frozen, they tend to break easily.

Variation Gently melt 2 oz. good quality semisweet chocolate and dip one end of each cooled cookie into the chocolate. Let set on nonstick parchment paper. Sprinkle the plain end with confectioners' sugar before serving.

Rich, traditional, and crumbly, these cookies were made to contrast with the privations of Lent, and echo the rich (and expensive) flavors of simnel cakes— dried fruit, butter, and spices or lemon.

easter cookies

1 stick unsalted butter, very soft

⅓ cup sugar

1 large egg yolk

the finely grated zest of
1 unwaxed lemon

1½ cups all-purpose flour

a good pinch of baking powder

a pinch of salt

⅓ cup golden raisins

Topping

1 egg white, lightly beaten

sugar, for sprinkling

*a fluted cookie cutter,
about 3 inches in diameter*

2 baking sheets, greased

Makes 16

Put the soft butter, sugar, and egg yolk in a bowl and beat with a wooden spoon, electric mixer, or whisk, until light and creamy. Beat in the lemon zest, then add the flour, baking powder, salt, and golden raisins. Mix with a wooden spoon. Bring the dough together with your hands. Wrap and chill until firm—about 20 minutes. At this point, the dough can be stored in the refrigerator for up to 3 days.

Roll out the dough on a floured work surface to about ¼ inch thick. Cut out rounds with the fluted cookie cutter. Arrange well apart on the prepared pans.

Bake in a preheated oven at 400°F for about 10 minutes until pale golden and firm.

Remove the trays from the oven, lightly brush each cookie with egg white, then sprinkle with a little sugar. Return to the oven and bake for a further 3–5 minutes or until the tops have become golden and crunchy.

Remove from the oven and let cool on the tray for 1 minute, then transfer to a wire rack to cool completely.

Store in an airtight container and eat within 5 days or freeze for up to a month.

Variation Omit the lemon zest. Add ½ teaspoon apple pie spice, ½ teaspoon ground cinnamon, and a good pinch of grated nutmeg to the flour. Use currants or raisins instead of the golden raisins, and add 1 teaspoon finely chopped mixed candied peel if you like.

These sweet, almond-rich cookies are like soft, chewy amaretti. Serve with coffee at the end of a special meal; a box of them makes a lovely gift.

sardinian wedding cookies

¾ cup (1 lb.) almond paste

⅔ cup slivered almonds, plus an extra ⅓ cup for sprinkling

2 large egg whites

a scant ½ cup confectioners' sugar

2 baking sheets lined with nonstick parchment paper

Makes 30

Break up the almond paste and put in a food processor. Process briefly until the paste is finely chopped. Add the almonds, egg whites, and sugar and process until the mixture forms a thick, smooth paste.

Using a tablespoon of mixture for each cookie, drop or spoon the mixture onto the prepared pans, spacing the cookies slightly apart. Sprinkle the remaining almonds over the top of the cookies.

Bake in a preheated oven at 300°F for about 25 minutes until light golden brown. Let cool completely on the trays, then remove the cookies. Store in an airtight container and eat within a week. These cookies don't freeze very well.

Variation Replace the almonds (in the mixture and for sprinkling) with pine nuts.

Traditionally made for the Christmas holidays, these dark, spicy cookies can be left plain or decorated with white frosting—you can use ready-made frosting writing pens for this.

swedish pepper cookies

1½ cups all-purpose flour

½ teaspoon baking soda

1 teaspoon ground cinnamon

1 teaspoon ground ginger

½ teaspoon ground black pepper

the freshly grated zest of 1 unwaxed orange

¾ cup sugar

1 stick unsalted butter, chilled and cut into small pieces

1 large egg, lightly beaten

1 tablespoon molasses

star-shaped cookie cutter

2 baking sheets, greased

Makes about 15

Put all the ingredients in a food processor and blend until the mixture forms a soft dough.

Remove the dough from the processor, wrap in plastic wrap or wax paper, and chill for 1 hour or until firm.

Lightly flour the work surface and a rolling pin and roll out the dough to about ¼ inch thick. Stamp out star shapes with the cookie cutter.

Arrange the shapes slightly apart on the prepared pans and chill for 10 minutes.

Bake in a preheated oven at 325°F for 10–12 minutes until dark golden brown and firm.

Let cool for 5 minutes, then transfer to a wire rack and let cool completely. Add decoration, if using (see recipe introduction). Store in an airtight container and eat within a week or freeze undecorated cookies for up to a month.

savory

Truly rich and crumbly, these savory cookies are hard to resist, and they rapidly disappear at parties. The cheese dough can be kept in the refrigerator for a week before baking, making for easy entertaining.

walnut cheddar shortbreads

1 cup all-purpose flour

1 stick unsalted butter, chilled and cut into small pieces

1 cup grated sharp Cheddar cheese

3 pinches of ground black pepper or cayenne

3 tablespoons walnut pieces

2 baking sheets, lightly greased

Makes 25

Put the flour, pieces of butter, grated cheese, and pepper in a food processor. Process just until the mixture looks like very coarse crumbs, then add the walnut pieces. Process again briefly, until the mixture forms a very soft dough. Remove the dough from the processor, put onto a piece of plastic wrap or wax paper, and shape into a brick about 4½ x 1½ x 2½ inches.

Wrap and chill until firm, about 1 hour. The dough can be kept in the refrigerator, well wrapped, for up to a week.

Using a large, sharp knife, slice the dough very thinly, about ¼ inch.

Arrange the slices slightly apart on the prepared pans and bake in a preheated oven at 350°F for about 12 minutes until the edges turn light brown. Let cool in the pan for a minute, then transfer to a wire rack to cool completely.

Store in an airtight container (these cookies are fragile) and eat within 3 days or freeze for up to a month.

Pronounced "poacha," these cheese-filled savory sesame cookies are a favorite with my Turkish friend Zeynep. Use feta cheese, ready cubed and marinated in oil and herbs or peppers, or another feta or similar cheese. Eat warm with soup or with drinks.

pogaca

1¾ cups self-rising flour

½ teaspoon sea salt

2 good pinches of hot red pepper flakes

½ teaspoon baking soda

½ cup olive oil

½ cup plain yogurt

3½ oz. feta cheese (drained weight), cut into 30 small pieces

1 egg yolk, beaten, to glaze

sesame seeds, for sprinkling

2 baking sheets, greased

Makes 30

Put the flour, salt, red pepper flakes, baking soda, oil, and yogurt in a food processor and blend until the mixture comes together to form a ball of soft but not sticky dough. Remove the dough from the processor, wrap in plastic wrap or wax paper, and chill for 1 hour.

Flour your fingers, then take about a heaping teaspoon of dough, roll it into a ball with your hands, then press it out to a thin disk about 2½ inches across. Put a cube of feta in the center, then fold the disk in half to make a half-moon shape. Press the edges together—don't worry if it is not neat. Repeat with the rest of the dough. Arrange the pogaca on the prepared pans, spacing slightly apart.

Brush the tops with beaten egg yolk, sprinkle with plenty of sesame seeds, then bake in a preheated oven at 350°F for 12–15 minutes until light golden brown.

Cool on the trays for a minute, then eat warm from the oven, or transfer to a wire cooling rack to cool completely.

Store in an airtight container in the refrigerator and eat within 24 hours, or freeze for up to a month. Warm gently before serving.

Though designed to eat with soft cheeses, particularly goat cheese, and strong, hard cheeses such as Stilton and Cheddar, these are also good with soups.

whole-wheat cookies

¼ cup whole-wheat pastry flour

½ teaspoon sea salt

½ teaspoon baking powder

½ cup old-fashioned oatmeal or rolled oats

1½ tablespoons sugar

7 tablespoons unsalted butter, chilled and cut into small pieces

½ teaspoon garam masala or mild curry powder

1 extra-large egg, lightly beaten

a cookie cutter, about 2½ inches in diameter

2 baking sheets, greased

Makes about 20

Put the flour, salt, baking powder, oats, sugar, butter, and garam masala or curry powder in a food processor. Blend for a few seconds until the mixture looks like coarse breadcrumbs. Add the beaten egg and process until the mixture comes together to make a firm dough.

Remove the dough from the processor, put onto a floured work surface and roll out to about ¼ inch thick. Cut out rounds with the cookie cutter. Knead the trimmings together, then re-roll and cut out more rounds.

Arrange the cookies slightly apart on the prepared pans, prick with a fork and bake in a preheated oven at 375°F for 12–15 minutes until slightly brown around the edges.

Let cool on the trays for 2 minutes, then transfer to a wire rack to cool completely.

Store in an airtight container and eat within a week or freeze for up to a month.

Variation To make Sweet Whole-Wheat Cookies, omit the garam masala or curry powder and increase the sugar to 3½ tablespoons.

It's hard to eat just one of these crisp, savory crackers, so they're perfect with drinks at party time, or with a bowl of soup. The recipe comes from Alyson Cook, who caters to the stars of Hollywood.

alyson's parmesan herb crisps

1¼ cups freshly grated Parmigiano Reggiano cheese

1 cup all-purpose flour

1 stick unsalted butter, chilled and cut into small pieces

½ teaspoon dried herbes de Provence

½ teaspoon Worcestershire sauce

2 tablespoons white wine (optional)

2 baking sheets, greased

Makes 50–60

Put all the ingredients in a food processor and blend until the mixture forms a ball of dough.

Remove the dough from the processor and put on a sheet of nonstick parchment paper. Shape into a log about 12 x 1 inch.

Wrap tightly, then chill until firm, about 2 hours. The mixture can be kept in the refrigerator for up to 4 days.

When ready to cook, preheat the oven to 375°F. Cut the log into ¼-inch slices.

Arrange the slices well apart on the prepared pans and bake in the heated oven for 12–15 minutes until light golden brown.

Let cool on the trays for 2 minutes, then transfer to a wire rack to cool completely. Store in an airtight container and eat within 5 days or freeze for up to a month.

Crisp, crumbly Scottish oatcakes have been made for centuries and are still very popular. They are good with soft cheeses or strong Cheddars, or spread with butter and jam or honey. This recipe uses olive oil rather than the traditional lard, as well as fine oatmeal, available from natural food stores (note page 17).

oatcakes

1⅓ cups fine oatmeal, plus extra for rolling out

½ teaspoon sea salt

2 pinches of baking powder

3 tablespoons olive oil

½ cup minus 1 tablespoon boiling water

a round cookie cutter, about 2½ inches in diameter

2 baking sheets, greased

Makes about 16

Put the oatmeal, salt, baking powder, and olive oil in a food processor. With the motor running, pour in the boiling water through the feed tube. Process until the mixture just comes together. Remove the dough from the processor and put onto a work surface sprinkled with oatmeal. If the dough is very sticky, work in a little extra oatmeal—the dough soon firms up.

Roll out the dough to about ¼ inch thick, then cut out rounds using the cookie cutter. Knead the trimmings together, then re-roll and cut out more rounds.

Arrange the oatcakes slightly apart on the prepared pans and bake in a preheated oven at 325°F for about 15 minutes until the edges are lightly browned.

Let cool on the trays for 2 minutes, then transfer to a wire rack to cool completely.

Store in an airtight container and eat within a week or freeze for up to a month.

If the oatcakes become soft, they can be crisped up in the oven (heated as above) for 5 minutes.

Variations At the same time as the oatmeal, add either:
• 3 pinches of hot red pepper flakes to make Spicy Oatcakes
• 4 teaspoons poppy seeds or sesame seeds
• 1 tablespoon fresh thyme leaves.

index

conversion chart

Weights and measures are rounded up or
down slightly to make measuring easier.

Volume equivalents:

American	Metric	Imperial
1 teaspoon	5 ml	
1 tablespoon	15 ml	
¼ cup	60 ml	2 fl.oz.
⅓ cup	75 ml	2½ fl.oz.
½ cup	125 ml	4 fl.oz.
⅔ cup	150 ml	5 fl.oz. (¼ pint)
¾ cup	175 ml	6 fl.oz.
1 cup	250 ml	8 fl.oz.

Weight equivalents: Measurements:

Imperial	Metric	Inches	cm
1 oz.	25 g	¼ inch	5 mm
2 oz.	50 g	½ inch	1 cm
3 oz.	75 g	¾ inch	1.5 cm
4 oz.	125 g	1 inch	2.5 cm
5 oz.	150 g	2 inches	5 cm
6 oz.	175 g	3 inches	7 cm
7 oz.	200 g	4 inches	10 cm
8 oz. (½ lb.)	250 g	5 inches	12 cm
9 oz.	275 g	6 inches	15 cm
10 oz.	300 g	7 inches	18 cm
11 oz.	325 g	8 inches	20 cm
12 oz.	375 g	9 inches	23 cm
13 oz.	400 g	10 inches	25 cm
14 oz.	425 g	11 inches	28 cm
15 oz.	475 g	12 inches	30 cm
16 oz. (1 lb.)	500 g		
2 lb.	1 kg		

Oven temperatures:

110°C	(225°F)	Gas ¼
120°C	(250°F)	Gas ½
140°C	(275°F)	Gas 1
150°C	(300°F)	Gas 2
160°C	(325°F)	Gas 3
180°C	(350°F)	Gas 4
190°C	(375°F)	Gas 5
200°C	(400°F)	Gas 6
220°C	(425°F)	Gas 7
230°C	(450°F)	Gas 8
240°C	(475°F)	Gas 9